Robert A. M. Stern

by David Anger

Capstone Press

MINNEAPOLIS

Capstone Press • 2440 Fernbrook Lane • Minneapolis, MN 55447

Editorial Director   John Coughlan
Managing Editor   Tom Streissguth
Production Editor   James Stapleton
Book Design   Timothy Halldin

*Photo credits: Peter Aaron/ESTO Photographics: pp. 6, 7,
13, 16, 18, 22, 26, 28, 30, 31, 32, 34, 35, 37,; Peter
Aaron/ESTO Photographics/©The Walt Disney Company:
pp. 4, 8, 38, 41, 42; Ed Stoecklin: pp. 24, 25; Barbra Walz:
p. 10.*

Library of Congress Cataloging-in-Publication Data
Anger, David, 1963--
    Robert A. M. Stern / by David Anger
        p. cm. -- (Architects--artists who build)
    Includes bibliographical references (p. 44) and index.
    Summary: Describes the life and work of the noted
    American architect whose creations include Disney's
    animation studio.
    ISBN 1-56065-312-4
    1. Stern, Robert A.M.--Juvenile literature. 2. Architects--
    United States--Biography--Juvenile literature. [1. Stern,
    Robert A.M. 2. Architects.] I. Title. II. Series.
    NA737.S64A93   1996
    720'.92--dc20   95-23099
    [B]   CIP
                                               AC

Table of Contents

Chapter 1

An Animation Building for Disney

Have you ever wondered where the movies *Aladdin* and *The Lion King* were made? The answer is The Walt Disney Company's Feature Animation Building in Burbank, California.

This futuristic building shows the art, the fun, and the magic of **animation**. It is one of those rare buildings that makes people ask, "Can I come inside?"

Characters from Disney animated movies decorate the halls of the Feature Animation Building. *(Used by permission from The Walt Disney Company.)*

Hopeful actors try out at the Walt Disney Casting Center, designed by Robert Stern. *(Used by permission from The Walt Disney Company.)*

The Feature Animation Building holds Disney's animation secrets. Every day there are movies being made inside.

Disney asked Robert A.M. Stern to design a building that would capture the excitement of animation. Stern worked with the architects in his office. Together they created a remarkable place.

Passing the Feature Animation Building, you see Mickey Mouse's giant hat, covered with stars and a crescent moon. Big letters spell ANIMATION at the base of the hat. The letters look like those on the sign of a movie theater from the 1930s.

Below this sign is the building's entrance. Visitors walk into a sunny **rotunda**. The

Stern's Disney Yacht and Beach Club resort welcomes visitors with an imposing entrance. *(Used by permission from The Walt Disney Company.)*

security guard's desk there displays 5,000 pictures of the famous cartoon mouse.

From the rotunda, you enter the screening room. The ceiling of this room is covered with images of favorite Disney characters. The feature-film production departments lie beyond the screening room.

The Lion King, **Aladdin**, **and other Disney hits were created in the Feature Animation Building.** *(Used by permission from The Walt Disney Company.)*

Archives and computers are on the lower level. The post-production department, which includes the background department and **special effects** department, occupies the ground floor. The animation department is located on the second floor. The story development department is on the third floor.

All four floors are connected by a grand staircase. Each floor has its own "main street" or main hallway. On the main streets, the 700 people who work in the building can take a break and play a little. They can enjoy a game of ping-pong or even work out on an exercise machine.

Inside Mickey's hat is the office of Roy Disney, head of animation. Disney's desk is shaped like a crescent moon. A cabinet behind the desk recalls Mickey's hat, complete with stars.

Robert Stern's design of Disney's Feature Animation Building clearly isn't a typical office building.

Chapter 2

Discovering Architecture

Robert Stern's office is on the 18th floor of a building in midtown Manhattan, in New York City. From his office he can see the Statue of Liberty and the George Washington Bridge. These are familiar sights to Stern, who was born and raised in New York City. He has lived in New York most of his life, but it is still a thrill for him to look at the skyline of the city.

Stern was born on May 23, 1939. Franklin Roosevelt was president of the United States. New York's skyscrapers were already famous by this time. Postcards, newspapers, and movies had already made them familiar to the rest of the world.

Before World War I, the Woolworth Building was the tallest building to "scrape the sky" at 795 feet (238.5 meters). With it, the Age of the Skyscraper was born. As a youngster, Stern was amazed by two Manhattan skyscrapers—the Empire State Building and the Chrysler Building. Both were designed in the **Art Deco** style.

A Popular Style

The Art Deco style began in France and was popular in the 1920s. Skyscrapers in the Art Deco style were most often made of stone. Their roofs were often set back and rose up like mountains. Each skyscraper had special features that set it apart from others. Stern especially liked the Empire State Building, perhaps because it was the tallest office tower in the world–1,250 feet (325 meters).

The New York skyline didn't change much during the 1930s or during the time of World War II (1939-1945). In 1952 New York's first modern skyscraper–Lever House–opened.

Lever House looks like a glass prism. It is covered in green glass that reflects the sky.

Stern designed a modern expansion for the Mexx International headquarters, a classic building in Holland.

Stern saw that Lever House was a completely new kind of building. It is an example of **modern** architecture.

Like Art Deco, modern architecture came from Europe. The **Bauhaus**–a group of architects in Germany–invented modern architecture in the 1920s. They designed most of their buildings with flat roofs, and they used mostly glass and steel as building materials.

Exploring New York

Robert Stern always enjoyed drawing buildings and looking at them. When he was very young, he made many drawings of houses and cities. By the time he entered junior high school, he was exploring New York City and its buildings on his own. He would walk by the Empire State Building and Lever House. He was curious about the construction of a skyscraper being built across the street from Lever House. This was the Seagram Building, designed by Mies van der Rohe, a famous

German architect who had immigrated to America.

By this time Stern knew that he wanted to be an architect. On Saturdays, he would often visit the Museum of Modern Art, which had a famous architecture department.

In those days, when people heard of his interest in architecture, they would often ask Stern, "What do you think about Frank Lloyd Wright?" Stern had seen this famous architect walking down New York's Fifth Avenue. Wright was overseeing the construction of the Guggenheim Museum. With its long spiral ramp, the Guggenheim is one of the most original buildings of the 20th century.

Chapter 3

Becoming an Architect

Robert Stern's parents wanted him to get a broad education in different subjects before he began to study architecture. So, when he turned 18, Stern entered Columbia University in New York, where he studied American history.

After four years at Columbia, Stern went to Yale University in New Haven, Connecticut, to study architecture. On the Yale **campus** he

Stern knows the importance of carefully designing inside as well as exterior walls. Bright sunlight fills this hallway at the Disney Casting Center. *(Used by permission from The Walt Disney Company.)*

discovered many fascinating buildings. He especially liked the university's older, **Gothic**-style structures. They look like castles, with pointed arches and towering spires.

Campus Architecture

There were also examples of modern architecture on the campus. Stern's architecture

Stern designed this campus building for St. Paul's School in New Hampshire.

classes were held in one of these modern buildings, the Yale Art Gallery, designed by the famous American architect Louis Kahn. This building opened in the mid-1950s and, like many works of modern architecture, has floor-to-ceiling windows.

Stern's classes were led by Paul Rudolph, an important modern architect. Today, architecture students at Yale are taught in a newer building designed by Rudolph. It is a massive, nine-story structure with walls of rough concrete.

Postmodern Style

At Yale, Stern read the books of Robert Venturi. Like Stern, Venturi appreciated America's architectural history. He created an architectural style known as **postmodern**, meaning after the modern. This style applied old traditions to new buildings.

The postmodern style reacted against the bare glass-and-steel architecture of Mies van der Rohe and other modern architects. Postmodern architects favor stone and brick.

They often add to their buildings decorations like spires and arches. The postmodern style thrilled Stern. After graduating from Yale, he adopted many of its features.

In 1966, Stern worked as a designer in the office of Richard Meier. Then, in 1967, he formed a partnership with John Hagmann. The early buildings Stern designed, mostly houses, won much attention. People appreciated their bright colors, arched windows, curved walls, and porches.

By the mid-1970s, Stern's clients were asking him to design larger buildings. In 1977, he formed the firm he still heads, Robert A.M. Stern Architects. Here architects, landscape architects, interior designers, and support staff work together to design houses and also commercial and institutional buildings.

Architect and Author

Robert Stern is also a teacher and writer. He is a professor at Columbia University's Graduate School of Architecture, where he teaches historic and modern architecture. He

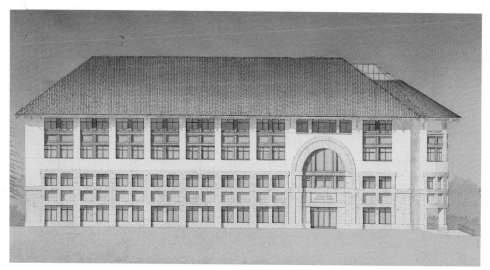

An artist's drawing shows the Gates Computer Center, one of Robert Stern's most recent projects. The center stands on the campus of Stanford University in California.

has written *New Directions in American Architecture,* a series of books about New York City, and even a book for young readers, *The House That Bob Built.* His book, *Pride of Place: Building the American Dream,* was published in 1986, when his popular television program of the same name made Stern one of America's best-known architects.

Chapter 4

Modern Traditionalism

Every architect creates buildings in a distinct style. Frank Lloyd Wright's buildings are horizontal and use a lot of wood. Mies van der Rohe stripped his buildings down to bare steel and smooth glass.

What is Robert Stern's style? His buildings are neither modern nor old. Instead, he blends the best of the past and the present. He calls his style Modern Traditionalism. Stern's architectural style often includes columns,

Stern uses a wide variety of geometric shapes to design the windows and roofs of private homes.

Stern has designed private homes, such as the Lang house, as well as commercial buildings.

wood shingles, **gabled** roofs, and arched windows.

Over the years Stern has designed many houses. He has also designed apartments, townhouses, and housing communities.

Stern's own house in East Hampton, New York, demonstrates his appreciation for the past and the present. A shingled cottage with a gabled roof, it is like an older house with many modern features.

A New Design

Stern relied on the architecture of yesterday when he designed the house. It looks like the summer houses built along the eastern seaboard at the turn of the century. But the cottage's design was also influenced by such 20th-century architects as Alvar Aalto, Robert Venturi, and Charles Moore.

The Lang residence signaled a change in Stern's style. Until this house was finished in

The flat roof and simple facade of the Lang house were unusual for a Stern design.

The Lawson Residence sits high on a sand dune, overlooking the ocean.

1972, most houses Stern designed were on Long Island, in New York. The Lang home is set in the rolling hills of Connecticut.

The Langs asked the architect to design a house that was not too expensive. This was a big challenge because construction costs and supplies are expensive. To meet their request, Stern kept the outside **facade** simple, with little decoration. He also made the rooms very simple.

Unlike most of Stern's designs, the Lang residence has a flat roof. The outside of the house has white molding and yellow walls. The back of the Lang house looks more modern than the front.

A large curved wall is the most important part of the design. Big windows are set in this wall. Inside, the ceilings are high and the rooms take full advantage of the large windows. There is also a round window at the rear, something found in many Stern designs.

One of Stern's favorite projects is the Lawson Residence. The house sits high on a sand dune that looks over the Atlantic Ocean. The house has sweeping views of the sea.

A high gabled roof covers the house's attic rooms, where a large arched window faces the ocean. In the kitchen, Stern placed a circular window within a square window. Downstairs, there are three guest rooms for weekend visitors.

Chapter 5

Major Projects by Robert Stern

Disney Casting Center
Walt Disney World
Lake Buena Vista, Florida
1987-1989

Applying for a job is never easy. Walt Disney World in Florida makes a hard task almost fun. Job-seekers report to Disney's Casting Center. The 60,000-square-foot (5,400-square-meter) Casting Center was designed by Robert Stern. Inside and out, the building

(Used by permission from The Walt Disney Company.)

Diamonds and pyramids decorate the Disney Casting Center at Walt Disney World in Florida.
(Used by permission from The Walt Disney Company.)

carries images from Disney movies and theme parks. The bronze handles of the front door, for instance, look like characters from *Alice in Wonderland.*

Visitors enter the building through a huge oval rotunda. In the rotunda there are 12 gold statues of Disney's most famous characters, including Mickey Mouse. **Murals** of Disney World cover a long, skylit hallway. At the end of the hallway, job-seekers enter the office where they begin the application process.

Mexx International
International Headquarters
Voorschoten, The Netherlands
1987

When officials from Mexx International asked Robert Stern to design an expansion of their international headquarters, the architect traveled to the Netherlands, where the company is based.

Stern fit a modern annex to a traditional structure at Mexx International.

In the town of Voorschoten, Stern visited Mexx's existing building, a 25,000-square-foot (2,250-square-meter) building from the mid-19th century. It sits on a large property like a huge estate.

New Rooms for an Old Company

Stern's design doubled the size of the company's headquarters. Behind the old structure, the new building adds a display area,

The expansion rises above a calm reflecting pool.

A wall of glass brightens Mexx International's new atrium.

meeting rooms, and office space. Together, the old and new buildings surround an atrium and a reflecting pool.

The Mexx International complex shows the contrast between the past and the present, the traditional and the modern. While the original building is reserved and classical, Stern's addition has many lighthearted and modern shapes. Yet the expansion fits smoothly into the building's overall design.

Disney's Yacht and Beach Club Resorts
Lake Buena Vista, Florida
1991

Many people who visit Walt Disney's Epcot Center in Florida stay at Disney's Yacht and Beach Club resorts. Stern designed the resorts with 1,215 guest rooms, a 110,000-square-foot

(Used by permission from The Walt Disney Company.)

The Yacht and Beach Club resorts (above and left) borrow from traditional resort architecture. *(Used by permission from The Walt Disney Company.)*

(9,900-square-meter) convention center, and a 35,000-square-foot (3,150-square-meter) fantasy pool.

Inspired by the Past

The design of the hotels was inspired by America's architectural past. The Yacht Club resembles the large, shingle-covered seaside resorts that were built in the last century in towns like Newport, Rhode Island, and Bar Harbor, Maine.

The Beach Club is lighter and more airy. It is modeled on the cottages and resorts of towns like Cape May, New Jersey.

Ohrstrom Library, St. Paul's School
Concord, New Hampshire
1991

Students at the St. Paul's School in New Hampshire don't mind studying, especially when they're studying in the Ohrstrom Library. The building looks very serious from the outside, but inside it is bright and comfortable.

Robert Stern visited the campus of St. Paul's School after receiving the assignment to design a new library. He looked at the site and at the buildings already on the campus. He then researched historic library buildings. The Crane Library in Quincy, Massachusetts, built in 1882, and others gave Stern ideas for the

Ohrstrom Library. His final design is a red-brick building that looks both traditional and modern.

The library incorporates up-to-date computer technology into traditional reading rooms. The central reading room is two stories high with big windows that open to a beautiful pond.

The Ohrstrom Library blends with older and traditional buildings on the St. Paul's campus.

Chapter 6

Advice from Robert Stern

Robert Stern says there is no formula for becoming an architect. He believes that young people should first learn to read well and write well.

For young people interested in a career in architecture, Stern says they must know and

An atrium at the Disney Feature Animation Building lends a futuristic air to a place where film magic is created. *(Used by permission from The Walt Disney Company.)*

love buildings and their surroundings. If you appreciate a particular skyscraper, you should ask, "What is it that makes this building special?" If you dislike a classroom at school, why not wonder, "What would make this room nicer?"

In Robert Stern's office they approach the process of designing a building in this way. First, Stern learns what the client's needs are–and what their dreams are, too. He challenges clients to imagine their dreams, even if their budget isn't big enough to accommodate all of their fantasies.

The Site Influences the Design

In the case of Disney's Feature Animation Building, The Walt Disney Company asked Stern to design a fun place. After talking about needs and dreams, Stern visited the location where the structure was to be built. He says that the site on which a building is to be built often shapes the design.

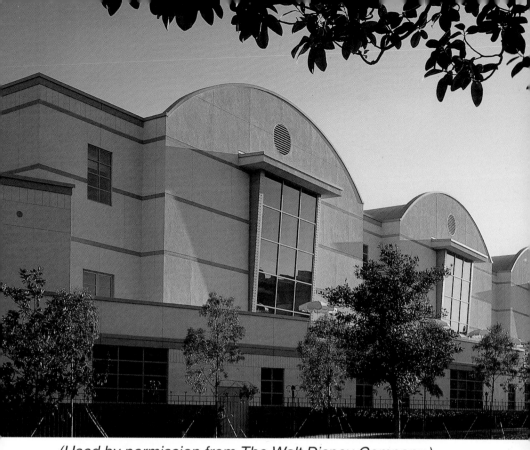

Robert Stern designs buildings all over the world. He has recently completed a number of projects, including the Norman Rockwell Museum in Stockbridge, Massachusetts; the Center for Jewish Life at Princeton University in Princeton, New Jersey; and hotels for Euro Disneyland near Paris, France. These days Robert Stern is working on the design of buildings in 12 states as well as Japan.

Glossary

animation–the work of making images on film from hand-drawn originals or from computer graphics

Art Deco–a decorative style of the late 1920s and 1930s, revived in the 1960s, based on geometric forms

Bauhaus–an important institute of architecture and design founded in Germany by Walter Gropius

(Used by permission from The Walt Disney Company.)

campus–the grounds of a school

facade–the face of a building, usually the front exterior

gable–a triangular wall section between the two slopes of a roof

Gothic style–an architecture style of western Europe from the 12th through the 15th centuries. Pointed arches, flying buttresses and ornamental carving mark the Gothic style.

modern architecture–describes a style of architectural design that uses simple shapes, light masses, and materials such as glass, concrete, and steel

mural–a large picture or decoration applied directly to a wall

postmodern architecture–a style that reacted against modern architecture and which exaggerates historical forms, like columns and cornices

rotunda–a circular hall, especially one with a dome

special effects–visual effects used to create illusions in motion pictures

To Learn More

Anger, David. *Cesar Pelli.* Minneapolis: Capstone Press, 1996.

Darling, David. *Spiderwebs to Skyscrapers: The Science of Structure.* New York: Dillon Press, 1991.

Horwitz, Elinor Lander. *How to Wreck a Building.* New York: Pantheon, 1992.

Kudalis, Eric. *Michael Graves.* Minneapolis: Capstone Press, 1996.

_____ *Gyo Obata.* Minneapolis: Capstone Press, 1996.

Stern, Robert A.M. *Pride of Place: Building the American Dream.* Boston: Houghton Mifflin, 1986.

_____ *The House That Bob Built.* New York: Rizzoli International, 1991.

Wadsworth, Ginger. *Julia Morgan: Architect of Dreams.* Minneapolis: Lerner Publications Company, 1990.

Some Useful Addresses

American Institute of Architects (AIA)
  Careers Program
1735 New York Avenue
Washington, DC 20006

Frank Lloyd Wright Foundation
Taliesin West
Scottsdale, Arizona 85261

National Building Museum
401 F Street NW
Washington, DC 20001

National Organization of Minority
  Architects
Howard University
School of Architecture and Planning
2366 Sixth Street
Washington, DC 20059

Some Buildings Designed by Robert A. M. Stern

California
Police Headquarters Building, Pasadena

Connecticut
The Shops at Somerset Square, Glastonbury

Florida
Walt Disney World Casting Center and Walt
  Disney World Yacht and Beach Club
  Resorts, Lake Buena Vista

Massachusetts
The Norman Rockwell Museum,
  Stockbridge

New Hampshire
Ohrstrom Library, St. Paul's School,
  Concord

New Jersey
Classical Pool Pavilion, Deal
Princeton University, The Center for Jewish
  Life, Princeton

New York
Kol Israel Synagogue, Brooklyn
Brooklyn Law School, Brooklyn
42nd Street Development Project,
  Manhattan

Virginia
Observatory Hill Dining Hall,
  University of Virginia, Charlottesville

France
Euro Disneyland Hotel Cheyenne and
  Newport Bay Club Hotel, Marne la Vallee

The Netherlands
Mexx International Headquarters,
  Voorschoten

Index